I Did It

I Did It

Harlow Rockwell

Ready-to-Read

Aladdin Books
Macmillan Publishing Company
New York

Aladdin Books
Macmillan Publishing Company
866 Third Avenue, New York, NY 10022
Collier Macmillan Canada, Inc.

First Aladdin Books edition 1987
Printed in the United States of America

10   9   8   7   6   5   4   3   2

LIBRARY OF CONGRESS CATALOGING-IN-PUBLICATION DATA
Rockwell, Harlow.   I did it.
  Reprint: Originally published: New York :
Macmillan, 1974. Originally published in
series: Ready-to-read.
  Summary: Simple instructions for making a
variety of things from easily available materials.
Included are a paper bag disguise, a papier maché
fish, and bread.
  1. Handicraft—Juvenile literature.   [1. Handicraft]   I. Title.
TT160.R58 1987 745.5 86-22146 ISBN 0-689-71126-3 (pbk.)

for Hannah, Elizabeth
and Oliver

Contents

Someone Else

I took a big paper bag
and I cut out two little holes
with my scissors.

I took my crayons
and I drew two big eyes
around the little holes.
I drew a long, long nose
and a funny mustache.

I drew bushy eyebrows.
I drew a mouth
and big white teeth.
I drew ears
and hair.

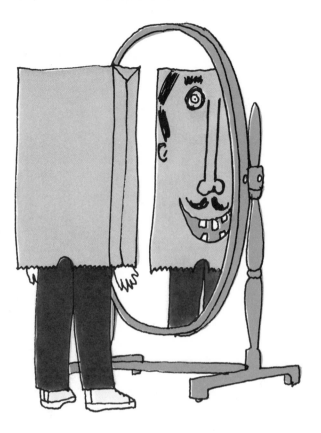

I put the paper bag
over my head.
I could see out of the
two little holes.
I looked in the mirror
but I did not see myself.
I saw someone else.

I went outside.

"Hello," I said

in a big, gruff voice.

No one knew me.

Everyone thought

I was someone else.

Then I was myself again.

And then Susan

was someone else.

Tiger

I saw some popcorn kernels

in the kitchen cabinet.

I saw dried kidney beans

and black beans

and white navy beans

and green split peas.

"I can make something with these,"

I said to my mother.

"Soup," she said.

"No. You wait and see," I said.

And I took the dried peas
and beans and popcorn
to my room.
I found my glue.

I found a piece of cardboard
and my pencil.
I drew something
on the cardboard.
It was a tiger.

I put glue on the stripes.

I put black beans in the glue.

I made black stripes.

I made eyes
with black beans and white beans.
I made a black bean nose.
I made a mouth
of red kidney beans.

And under my tiger's nose
and around his mouth
I put white beans.
Then I put kernels
of yellow popcorn
everywhere there were no
stripes, eyes, nose, or mouth.
I used up a lot of glue.

"He needs a jungle,"
I said to myself.
I made a jungle
of green split peas.
And then my tiger
was done.

"Look what I did,"
I said to my mother.
"What a beautiful tiger," she said,
and put him on the bookcase.
I see him there
every day.

Fat Fish

I tore long strips of newspaper.

I made a lot of strips.

I put one cup of flour

and one cup of water

in a pot.

I stirred them.
I cooked them
until there were bubbles
and the mixture got thicker.
Then it was paste.
The paste cooled in the pot.

I blew up a balloon
and tied it.
It was big.

When the paste was cool
I put a strip
of newspaper in it.
Then I took out the strip
and stuck it on the balloon.

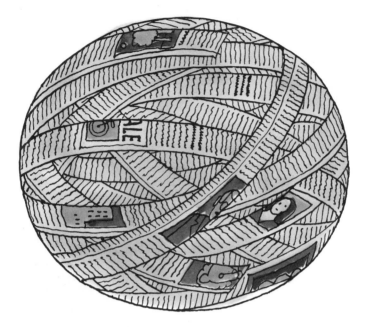

I stuck on some more,

and more,

and more.

I could not see my balloon.

I cut two cardboard triangles
and stuck them on
with paste and strips.
The paste and newspaper strips
dried on my balloon.

Next day, I poked it
with my fingernail.
It was hard.
I painted it green
and I could not see
the newspaper any more.

I painted a mouth.

I painted two eyes.

I painted two fins.

I painted some scales.

The two triangles made a tail.

I made a fat fish.

Jet

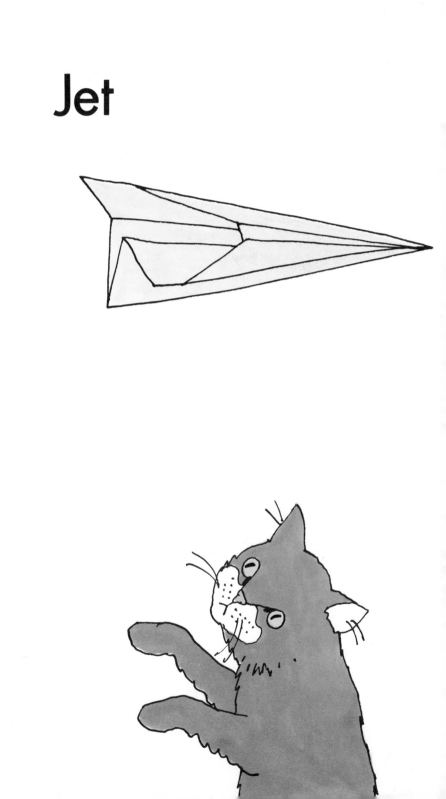

I got a piece of paper.

It was a rectangle.

I folded it this way.

That made a skinny rectangle.

I opened it up.

I folded it this way.

I made a triangle.

I made another triangle

on the other side.

I folded it this way.

I do not know

what kind of shape it was.

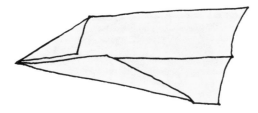

I did it again

on the other side.

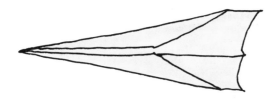

I folded it together again,

like this.

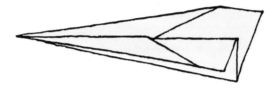

Then I folded it this way.

I turned it over.

I folded it this way again.

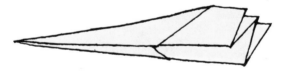

I picked it up.

I held it like this.

"Zoom!" I said.

I threw it.

It flew.

I made a jet.

Secret Message

There was half a lemon
in the refrigerator.
"That is just what I need,"
I said to myself.
I squeezed the lemon into a cup.

I made juice.

I took a toothpick

and dipped it in the lemon juice.

I wrote some words

in my notebook.

I wrote them with lemon juice

and a toothpick.

The words dried

and I could not see them any more.

No one could see them.

The words were secret.

I tore the page
out of my notebook.
I gave it to my father.
"Read this," I said.

"There is nothing
   on this paper,"
   said my father.
"I cannot read words
   I cannot see."
"It is a secret message,"
   I said.
"Hold the paper
   up to a light bulb
   where it is hot.
   But be careful!
   Do not burn your fingers."

My father held the paper
up to a light bulb.
It was hot.

Slowly,

slowly,

the words turned brown.

And my father read

the secret message.

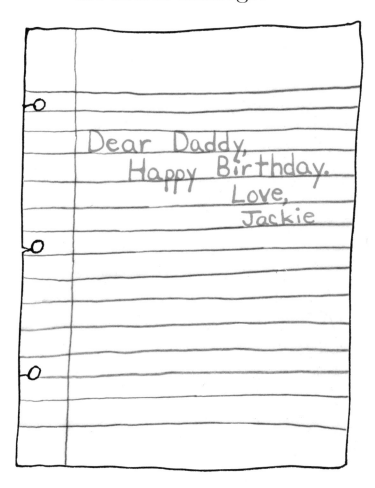

Two Loaves

I poured
one and a half cups
of warm water
into the big mixing bowl.
I added a teaspoon of salt
and a package of dry yeast.
I stirred.

I added a cup of flour.

I stirred.

I added three more cups of flour

and stirred some more.

I made dough.

I sprinkled some flour
on the kitchen table.
I put the dough on the table.
I folded the dough toward me
like this.

And then I pushed it away,
like this.

I kneaded the dough.
I kneaded for ten minutes.
Then I put the dough in the bowl.

I covered the bowl
with a warm, damp dishtowel.
And then I went outside
to play.

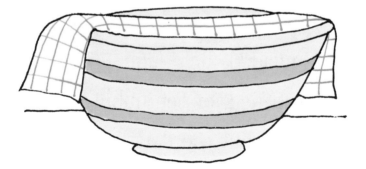

Two hours later
I looked at the dough.
There was more of it.
The dough was
twice as big
as it was before!

I punched the dough down
with my fist.
It was full of bubbles
and it squished
like an old balloon.

I smeared some cooking oil

on a cookie sheet.

I made two round balls

of dough.

I put them on the cookie sheet.

I read a book,

and drew a picture,

and played with my dog.

Forty-five minutes later

I looked.

The balls of dough

were bigger.

I turned on the oven

to three hundred and fifty degrees.

In fifteen minutes

I put the cookie sheets

with the balls of dough

into the oven.

In forty minutes

I smelled something good.

The balls of dough

were big and brown.

They were not soft any more.

They were loaves of bread now.

I took the bread out of

the oven.

Everybody ate some
while it was still warm.
Now I am a baker.
I made bread.